Gisela Bulla

Fancy Rats

Photographs: Christine Steimer
Illustrations: György Jankovics

2 CONTENTS

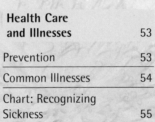

TYPICAL
FANCY RAT

- Intelligent and adaptable

- Afraid of loud noise

- Fond of dim light

- Bright-eyed and alert

- Good-natured and friendly

- Eager eaters

- Like to chew wood

- Gregarious and peaceable

- Homebodies

- Quick to mature and very prolific

- Available in various colors

Fancy rats are clever, adaptable, and endowed with a highly developed social instinct. These characteristics make fancy rats popular house pets. These pets develop an affectionate relationship with their people. They can learn to come when called. You can even take a rat along in the sleeve or pocket of a jacket when you go for a walk. Your fancy rat, happy to be with you, ordinarily won't be tempted by this opportunity to escape. Rats best display their entire spectrum of interesting behavior when they are kept with other rats.

IS A FANCY RAT FOR YOU?

1 Rats aren't for everyone. Does every member of the family feel comfortable with the new housemate? Is anyone put off by the idea of having a rodent as a pet?

2 Is any family member allergic to animal hair? (See Important Notes, page 63.)

3 Rats need physical contact with their owner. They are really happy if they can interact with their keeper. Are you prepared to hold the animal on your lap or carry it around in your sweater, up your sleeve, or on your shoulder?

4 Do you have the time and financial resources to care for your pet and have it treated by the vet if it should become ill?

5 Daily care—feeding, playing with your fancy rat, and cleaning its cage—takes time. Do you have enough?

6 Living animals are not toys; their life-style doesn't always parallel yours! Rats are especially active at dusk but like to sleep during the day without being disturbed. Can you adjust to this?

7 Rats gnaw on everything they can reach. As a result, you may experience some damage to your belongings while a rat takes its necessary daily free exercise.

8 You have to be careful and understanding if you have other house pets; not every pet is good company for your pet rat (see page 21)

9 The cage must be roomy and airy, and it must contain some hiding places. It must always be kept in the same place in the home.

10 Is there someone willing to take care of the pet when you're ill or on vacation?

Two Rats Are Better than One

In the wild rats are pack animals. Therefore, it's not advisable to have just one pet fancy rat, even if your intention is to be actively involved in caring for a single animal. A human can never take the place of another animal.

It's a good idea to keep two rats. If you have a breeding pair, though, you have to be ready to deal with dozens of rats in your house in a short time. Rats mature early and are *extremely* prolific.

Two young females usually get along just fine for as long as they live. Unfortunately, it's not so easy to determine the sex of young animals. Even pet store owners and experienced rat aficionados can be mistaken. So as soon as you get an animal, it's best to go straight to the veterinarian. Although reputable pet stores and breeders usually exchange a healthy animal, you should get a written agreement that specifies the animal's sex, and that permits exchange.

Note: Usually there are no fundamental differences in the way lone male and female rats act. Both are equally friendly. The male may grow to be a little larger. Two mature males in the same cage might not get along.

CHOOSING A FANCY RAT

It's indicative of the rat's intelligence that after thousands of years of persecution by humans it has gained the trust of its former enemies and turned into an affectionate pet through proper, loving care.

The Rat Finds a Friend

All over the world rats have been regarded as disgusting creatures and carriers of dangerous diseases—as indeed they have been. As a result they have been persecuted as vermin—hunted with dogs, shot for sport, and killed with poison. But anyone who takes a close look at rats realizes that they are not only intelligent and adaptable creatures, but also extremely lovable and affectionate house pets.

A rat that's kept as a house pet and handled lovingly quickly develops confidence in its caretaker, and in the process it demonstrates some remarkable behavior.

Black and Brown Rats

The ancestors of all fancy rats that are kept as house pets today are brown rats *(Rattus norvegicus)*. Two hundred years ago they came to Europe from China. The black rat *(Rattus rattus)* also came from Asia; presumably it had already migrated during prehistoric times.

Originally rats were widespread only in Asia, Europe, and Australia. The black rat was intro-

Tree trunks are a natural attraction for rats. They're good for climbing and gnawing.

duced into North America in the 16th century. Brown rats came to America as stowaways on ships, hidden among the cargo in the 18th century. That's how rats have managed to populate the entire world. Black and brown rats are different from one another and even occupy different habitats.

The black rat has a slender body, large thin nearly hairless ears, and large eyes. Its body is about six to nine inches long (16–24 cm), and its tail is from seven to ten inches long (18–25 cm).

Once black rats lived in trees, but as they became associated with humans, they moved into attics in houses and haylofts in barns.

The brown rat has a stocky robust body, small round furry ears, and small eyes. Its body is about eight to eleven inches long (21–28 cm), and the tail is six to nine inches long (16–24 cm). Brown rats live close to the ground.

Living in close proximity with humans, they inhabit basements of houses, and frequent sewers.

Rats Are Large Mice

Both the black rat *(Rattus rattus)*, which has been nearly exterminated in many places, and the brown rat *(Rattus norvegicus)* belong to the order of rodent (Rodentia), and to the most numerous family of true mice and rats *(Murinae)*, a sub-family of *Muridae*. Rats are distinguished from their smaller relatives, the mice, especially by the size of their body, their intelligence, and their smaller ears in proportion to body size. Even though rats belong to the same family, they can't stand mice. They chase them relentlessly and often kill them.

The Black Death

For almost four hundred years, from 1348 to 1740, the Black Death or bubonic plague infested Europe. At least 25 million people—approximately a third of the population at the time—fell victim to the plague. This fearsome scourge was attributed exclusively to the black rat. Today it is known that at least 250 different animals, most of which are rodents, can transmit this disease to people. Many types of animals infect people directly; however, rats can communicate the plague only by means of the rat flea, which must be infected with the plague pathogen *Yersinia pestis*. In addition, bubonic plague is communicable directly from person to person.

The plague may have been introduced into Europe as flea-infested black rats migrated from Italy throughout Europe. It could also have been introduced by ships' passengers already infected with the disease.

Where to Get a Fancy Rat

Since rats have become popular as house pets, they are available as fancy rats in pet stores. It's even worthwhile to ask at animal shelters, for rats are among the unfortunate pets whose owners, unable or unwilling to care for them, relinquish them to an uncertain fate. Local humane societies can often provide addresses of rat owners who can provide additional help. The same is true for veterinarians who are familiar with pet rats; they too can supply much solid information.

Fancy rats stand on their hind legs to reach a treat.

What to Look For

It's fairly easy for even a lay person to evaluate the health of a rat.

The animal's eyes should be clear, and under no circumstances stuck shut or inflamed.

The anal region should not be smeared with droppings. Healthy rats clean themselves very thoroughly. Only sick animals neglect their grooming.

The fur should be smooth; it should look clean and show no bald patches, scabs, or matted spots.

Behavior is also indicative of the animal's health. A healthy rat curiously approaches the cage bars whenever it has a visitor. Sick animals seem disinterested and apathetic. Young animals are friendly as long as they have had no traumatic experiences with humans.

Fur Colors

Brown rats living in the wild are wild-colored, also referred to as *agouti*, ranging in shading from grayish brown to reddish brown. Albinos, the preferred laboratory rats (the descendants of the black rat), have white fur and pink eyes. But there are also white rats with dark eyes.

Black-colored rats are fairly rare; white ones dappled with brown or black are more common. If only the head is dark, the rat is described as black-, red-, or auburn-hooded. They can be obtained from pet dealers.

Wild-colored rats are the most robust and lively. Because of genetic changes in metabolism, white dappled rats have a tendency to put on weight. Differences in behavior related to fur color have never been identified.

Note: In England, Germany, the United States, and many other places, fanciers have begun breeding pet or fancy rats in a variety of colors. There are beige rats with curly fur (fur and whiskers are kinky), or that are designated as "husky" and colored like a Siberian Husky dog. Recently rat clubs and societies have established rat standards that specify precisely how an animal should look. In my opinion, breeding rats for beauty alone is misguided, especially since there are more than enough rats already. The longer life expectancy that amateur breeders have sought in rats may not be achievable. In old books it's stated that the normal life expectancy of a rat is between six and seven years, but today that figure is dubious, because females reach menopause and become barren at the age of a year and a half. Compared with other rodents, it would then seem to have half its life behind it.

Rats are by nature very curious.

PORTRAITS:
FANCY RATS

The original grayish-brown to reddish wild color of rats has been modified through breeding. So today people can find fancy rats of many different colors in pet stores.

A chubby black and white dappled rat.

These wild-colored (agouti) rats, above and left, are similar in type to the original Eurasian brown rat.

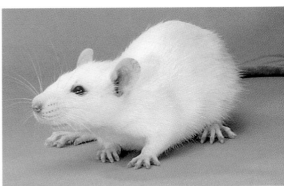

Photo at left: Mother and child. Wild-colored rat and hooded rat in black and white.

Photo top right: An Albino rat lacks pigment in coat and eyes.

Photo above: All-brown rats are attractive, and their pigmentation is chocolate in color.

Photo at right: Hooded rat in cream and white.

Legal Considerations

For renters: Small animals usually can be kept without express permission from the landlord, as long as ownership is not specifically forbidden in the rental contract. Unfortunately, that doesn't necessarily apply to rats. Some landlords may refuse permission to keep rats on their property. The animal must be removed upon demand.

In a condominium pet ownership can be forbidden by vote of condominium owners.

Pet owners' liability: Pet owners are responsible for all damages caused by their animals. Therefore it is advisable to leave rats in their cage if you are not present.

Commercial law: Although reputable breeders and pet store owners will usually exchange a pet on request, it's a good idea to get a written agreement that specifies that you have a right to exchange if you get a mating pair instead of two animals of the same sex, or if someone sells you a sick animal. Both matters are best clarified by visiting the veterinarian within 48 hours after purchase.

The Right Age at Purchase

Young rats should be at least four weeks old, and it's better if they're six weeks old. Younger animals have not had enough warmth in the nest and mother's milk, and that can lead to psychological and health problems.

Mother rats are very concerned about their young and care for them lovingly. The young should be allowed to benefit from this care for at least four weeks. Adult and half-grown rats can be moved to a new home at any age.

A Comfortable Home

Ask about rat cages when you purchase your pet. If none specifically designed for rats are available, consider a large hamster, chinchilla, or bird cage. The cage should not be made of wood; otherwise, the rat will quickly chew an exit for itself. A cage for two rats should be at least 31 inches long, 18 inches wide, and about 28 inches deep (80 × 45 × 70 cm), and it should have two stories. It is advisable to thoroughly clean a new cage as the coating commonly used on wire bird cages is toxic to rats.

Unfortunately, most of the cages you find in stores are too bright and airy. Rats like to hide, and prefer to sleep in the dark. That's why it's a good idea to line the cage on the sides and the top; experience shows that

Rats have an amazing sense of balance. They stow away on ships and disembark by running up and down the lines as the craft are made fast to the pier.

chipboard is best, and that the rats will seldom gnaw on it.

The front of the cage should be only half lined. It's best to nail the chipboard at the joints to construct a hood that you can slide over the cage as needed.

Note: There are special cages available at pet stores that make ideal living quarters for rats. They are about 29 × 30 × 29½ inches (74 × 76 × 75 cm). The sides are paneled with chipboard. Only the roof and part of the front are lined (see drawing, page 18). If any parts are wood, they must be replaced with chipboard.

Interior Design

Your fancy rat's cage should be divided into several living spaces.

In the wild brown rats live in underground dens with lots of passageways and chambers at various levels. The rooms are used for different purposes. There are sleeping, playing, living, and birthing rooms, a storage room, and a space for urinating and defecating.

In the cage rats should have at least a roomy living room and playroom, a bedroom with a sleeping house, and a bathroom. A birthing room is not mandatory, if you are not interested in breeding, and the storage room is unnecessary because you give the rats fresh food every day.

The cage should be divided into two or three stories,

ideally with chipboard. The rats get from one level to another by means of firmly attached ladders or metal ramps and ceramic tubes available in pet stores. Additional access is provided by holes the size of a silver dollar that are cut into the floors. In general, the cage should be as complex as possible on the inside. You can accomplish that by installing chipboard partitions with doorways cut in them. Only the living room and the playroom should be spacious.

Aquariums and Terrariums

Glass-sided tanks are not ideal rat houses. The slick walls afford the animals no climbing opportunities, and if the walls are higher than 14 inches (35 cm), the air exchange is insufficient. For that reason, ladders, seesaws, and passageways are especially important accessories inside the cage. Of course, aquariums and terrariums must be draped on the outside, since rats like darkness.

Note: Rats can be perfectly comfortable in simple homemade boxes of laminated chipboard. There should be a large wire mesh door on the front and two stories inside.

Where Should the Cage Be Placed?

The cage must be kept in a single place in the home; it must not be dragged back and forth between locations. The best place is a quiet corner protected from sunlight, cold, and draft. Rats are very sensitive to draft, low temperatures, and excessive heat.

Cage Accessories

Pine Bedding

Bedding (pine wood shavings) from the pet store is the best choice for rats. Straw, peat moss, hay, and pelletized straw are suitable as long as they're guaranteed to be free of chemical sprays. Rats sometimes can have a reaction to natural straw or hay and you run the risk of introducing mites and insects. In that case, the rats scratch themselves frequently, and develop bloody or scabby patches in their fur. Dispose of the contaminated bedding immediately, wash the cage, and disinfect both it and the area around the cage with a flea spray.

Rats, which like the dark, feel at home in this cave made of tree bark.

Note: Place a thick layer of newspaper or wrapping paper on the cage floor underneath the bedding. Rats shred the paper, producing a second absorbent layer next to the bedding, and that helps reduce the urine odor. Since printer's ink is lead-free, it presents no danger of poisoning the animals. When you use newspapers, sometimes the ink is partially dissolved by urine and rats get ink spots on their coats—unsightly, but harmless. If you want to avoid that, you should use paper towels.

Sleeping House

The sleeping house needs to be large enough to accommodate two full-grown rats. Guinea pig houses or rabbit houses meet this requirement best; they are available in pet stores. Appropriate materials are stainless steel, ceramic, or hard plastic (see drawing on page 19). The best location for the sleeping house is in a quiet corner on the top floor of the cage.

Note: Paper towels, fabric remnants, and hay (see Pine Bedding, page 16) are the best material for lining the sleeping house. Rats shred paper into tiny bits. This type of behavior satisfies the natural nest-building instinct.

Food Dishes and Water Bottles

It's a good idea to buy two food dishes: one for pellets, and the other for fresh green feed and fruits (see page 30). The dishes should be glazed stoneware, about five inches (12 cm) across.

A gravity-feed or valve-type eight-ounce water bottle with a drinking spout, like the ones used for rabbits and guinea pigs, can be bought in pet stores and hung on the cage bars. Be sure that the bottle and lid are made of glass or plastic. Rubber stoppers make the water unpalatable.

Place an additional water bowl with a secure base on the top floor of the cage.

Note: Food and water dishes should not be placed in a corner, but away from the edges of the cage; otherwise the rats might use them as their toilet area, contaminating the food and water.

Checklist
What to Buy

1 A cage with a surface area at least 32 inches by 18 inches, and 28 inches high (80 x 45 x 70 cm), with a cover made of chipboard (see page 14)

2 A ceramic or plastic sleeping house

3 Two stoneware food dishes— 7 inches (17 cm) diameter—and a water bottle with drinking spout to hang on cage bars

4 Bedding for the cage floor: a layer of hamster bedding or pine chips a little more than an inch (3 cm) thick
Newspaper, packing paper, or paper towels as a bottom layer

5 Material for lining the sleeping house: paper towels, hay, or straw

6 For climbing: metal ladders and ramps, ceramic or plexiglas tubes, or climbing ropes from the pet store

7 For playing: wooden seesaws, paper balls, and cardboard tubes

8 For gnawing: hard bread crusts, nuts in shells, and twigs from deciduous trees

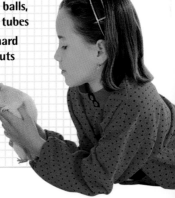

Transport

A plastic travel cage or a bird cage keeps your fancy rat safe and secure on the trip home. You can use the cage later to take the rats to the veterinarian. The cage should be large enough to permit two rats to lie down. Place an old magazine on the floor and cover it with bedding or paper towel.

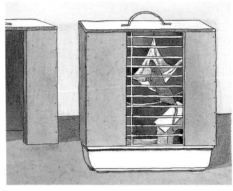

A chipboard hood slips over the cage, providing the darkness that rats need.

This small crate with a view is ideal for transporting your pet.

Cardboard boxes with airholes are not escape-proof.

Preparations for the Move

Before the new residents move in, the cage and accessories should be set up in the place where they will remain (see A Comfortable Home, page 14). Also securely fasten one or two fairly thick branches for climbing in the living room.

The pet store owner should give you a small quantity of the food the rat has been eating. That makes the transition easier, even though the rats will probably like the food you provide for them.

Making Friends with Rats

When you get home, devote some time to the

Rats Like Quiet

Fancy rats become nervous and might panic if they're disturbed by loud music, a barking dog, noisy children, slamming doors—in short, any kind of noise. By nature, rats have a strong preference for quiet. At the start, when your animal is not used to you and its new surroundings, it's important to avoid making noise. That's the only way the rats will settle in quickly and develop trust in you.

fancy rats. If you put them into the cage right away, they'll probably hide and not come out again for some time. That's especially true for timid animals. The most important thing for rats is physical contact with their owner. Sit on a chair in the room with the rats on your lap and form a roof over your lap with your hands to make a shelter where the rats can hide. That way they pick up your scent (avoid using cologne or scented soaps) and develop trust in you.

In this phase of adjustment, don't pet the animals; rather, speak softly and calmly to them. If a rat tries to run

*A plastic or ceramic sleeping house gives the rats a
sense of security.*

away, calmly place it back in your lap. If the
animals feel safe, they will fall asleep there. It's
a good idea to move the phone into another
room or take it off the hook.

After about an hour you can put the rats
into their cage. Be sure that the food dishes
and water bottle are filled. From the beginning
there should also be some nibbling material
available, such as a juicy carrot and some dried
bread.

Other family members and children must be
asked to exercise restraint in the early days
before the rats have become accustomed to the
new home. At first, admire the newcomers
through the cage bars, without sticking your
fingers into the cage, and keep other house
pets away.

Note: If the rats were bought for a child, he
or she should be the first to make friends with
the rats. Explain what to do and watch what
happens from a respectful distance. The young-

*Folding your hands like a roof over the
rat makes the animal feel secure and
permits the animal
to recognize your
personal scent.*

ster must know that fancy rats must never be
picked up by the tail, which could break off.

The following day the fancy rats can have
their first free exercise in the room. Close doors
and windows. If the rats don't want to leave
the cage, reach in carefully with your hand and
lift them out. When you do so, place your hand
under the animal's belly, right behind the front
legs, and put your thumb on its back. Then you
can place the rat on your lap again, or let it
explore the room (see Dangers, page 23). It's
important that you speak to the animals in a
soft voice. Leave the cage door open so that
the rats can go back in any time they wish.
Don't leave the room while they are out.

Turn off the TV

If your TV set is in the same room as your new
pets, turn it off while the fancy rats get used to
their new surroundings. The loud, strange voices
of news commentators might frighten your
pets, and the noise and vibrations from loud
explosions, police sirens, shouting, and canned
laughter on some TV programs will terrify them.
Keep the volume low on
your radio or stereo,
too. Studies have
shown that animals
prefer classical
music, so play some
Mozart to soothe
your fancy
rats.

It's easy to keep fancy rats. The important thing is to house them properly, feed them nutritious food, give them variety and attention, and spend enough time with them. Problems arise if the animals are neglected or handled roughly.

Children and Rats

In general, rats are not suitable playmates for children under twelve, for they may bite if they are picked up clumsily. In any case, children need to observe certain rules.

✔ Never grab or lift a rat by the tail. The animal will react in panic and might bite. The sensitive tail breaks easily—an extremely painful injury. Treatment by a veterinarian is absolutely necessary in such cases.

✔ Do not disturb fancy rats when they are sleeping—not even to feed them or to play with them.

✔ Don't fill rats up with snacks between meals. The rats would like it, but they would quickly get fat. Obesity can be harmful to their health.

✔ When the rats are running free, walk very carefully to avoid hurting them. Doors, windows, and drawers must be closed.

✔ The best playtime for rats is in the evening or early morning.

Rats are very clean animals. Several times every day they lick their fur clean.

Rats and Other Pets

Some dogs can get used to rats. But if your dog is a terrier, Dachshund, Miniature Pinscher, or any other breed originally developed to hunt small prey, don't get a rat as a pet. Your dog should be calm, since rats are highly sensitive to noise and are stressed by barking dogs. Help your dog understand that the rat is part of the family and is off limits. At first the dog should only sniff at the newcomer through the cage bars. Explain to it quietly that the rat is there to stay. When you are holding the rat on your lap, the dog should be allowed to sniff it. If the dog behaves itself, praise it. Pet both animals and praise them. Allow the animals together only under supervision. If the rat shows any signs of fear, keep the pets apart.

Cats: Making an adult cat understand that the rat is not a prey animal is a real trick. In some cases this has worked, but it's not recommended. It's another thing, though, if a rat is introduced to a young kitten about eight weeks old. Since the kitten's urge to play is highly developed, it might accept the rat as a playmate. If the two make friends, you can let them romp around together. If it gets to be too much for the rat, it will retreat into its cage.

Always leave the cage door open during free exercise. If the kitten won't leave the rat alone, but keeps scratching at the cage, put it into another room. Always supervise play between the cat and the rat.

Mice: Don't keep mice and rats at the same time, or at least keep them in separate rooms. Rats consider mice prey.

Hamsters: The solitary hamster shuns even its own kind. It couldn't care less about a rat. On the other hand, the rat probably would kill a hamster if given the opportunity.

Rabbits: Very active rabbits will chase a rat. One or the other will be injured.

Birds are prey animals to rats. Even if the birdcage is set up in such a way that the rat can't reach it, it will always try, and the bird will live in continual fear. For that reason, the bird should be housed in a different room. And don't schedule the bird's free flights at the same time as the rat's free exercise.

Fish: An aquarium should always have a good cover, for the brown rat is especially clever at fishing.

Rat Meets Rat

If you want to get a companion for an adult rat that has been raised alone, the only possibility is a young animal of the same sex. A young animal will be accepted better by an adult female than by a male, which might consider it a rival and kill it.

✔ Don't put the new animal into the cage with the other one right away.

✔ Both rats must have the opportunity to get to know each other and pick up each other's scent.

✔ Place a smaller cage with the young animal in it near the larger cage containing the established rat. That way the two of them can watch each other and sniff each other from a safe distance.

✔ Take the little rat onto your lap frequently and pat it with your hands so that it picks up and gets used to your scent too.

✔ Then let both rats have free exercise together in the house. Supervise the process.

✔ When the two rats have become friends, attempt to place them both in the large cage.

✔ Watch to see if the animals act peacefully.

✔ If they fight, the rats have to be separated.

In the wild, rats are very tolerant of one another as long as they belong to the same extended family. Strangers from a different burrow with a different scent are driven off. If they have no escape route—as in a closed cage—the intruder is killed following a lengthy warning.

The harassed rat may save its hide if it utters the "humility cry" in high-frequency tones imperceptible to humans in the 20–25 kHz range. That signifies surrender, which is always accepted by experienced rats. But this cry of humility is not inborn; it must be learned

When you pick up and carry a grown rat, hold the animal firmly under the chest and over the back while you support its hindquarters with your other hand.

Avoid Dangers to Your Fancy Rat

Danger	Source	How to Avoid
Escape	Doors, windows	Close doors and windows when rats are running around free.
Getting Pinched	Doors, cabinet doors, drawers	Keep closed.
Electric Shock	Electric cords, wall sockets	Run wires in walls, pull plugs, block outlets with safety plates, eliminate exposed cords.
Heatstroke	Sun, heaters	Don't place the cage in direct sun or near heaters.
Cold Shock	Temperatures under 46°F (8°C)	Rats are very sensitive to cold. Don't turn the heat down too low in the winter.
Burns	Candles, burning cigarettes, stove pipes, stove, and toaster	Extinguish candles, don't leave burning cigarettes, don't light the wood stove. Unplug stove and toaster or shut kitchen door.
Poisoning	Poisonous plants and cleaning agents, alcohol, cigarettes and butts	Remove poisonous plants, keep alcohol and cigarettes in cabinets, don't leave butts in ashtrays, clean cage with hot water and vinegar.
Contusions	Accidentally getting stepped or sat on	Move carefully when the rats are loose. Don't accidentally sit on an animal.
Internal Injuries	Small, sharp objects	Pick up needles, thumbtacks, nails, etc., so they can't be swallowed by the animal.

(see page 50). Rats raised for laboratory experiments and others that have been kept in isolation are unfamiliar with it.

Note: If you have an elderly male rat that's not expected to live much longer, I advise against experimenting with it. It won't get much pleasure from associating with a lively younger animal.

Running Free in the Home

Rats, which are most active in reduced light, are best suited to free exercise in the early morning and the evening. The more exercise your rat gets, the better. The minimum is an hour per day. If the animals are thoroughly settled in and everything is secure, you can let them run around all day. But you'll have to resign yourself to cleaning up droppings and urine. At night, shut the animals in their cage so they don't start to work on your upholstered furniture or gnaw on table legs.

You'll have to watch over the animal's free exercise, especially in the first three to four weeks, for several reasons:

1. The animal might hurt itself, or be injured through human carelessness.

2. Rats can cause considerable damage to furniture, upholstery, and cushions, since they continually need to wear away their incisors. If they try it, calmly take them away and give them something they can gnaw—a slice of hard, mold-free bread or a piece of wood.

3. Upholstered furniture and cushions stimulate rats to build nests. If they start to work on the upholstery, calmly place them on the floor or a table and give them a crumpled-up piece of paper in which a small treat is hidden. Rats are even happy to have an old piece of clothing or a discarded handkerchief. Pure cotton or linen are best, for they are harmless to the rats if they swallow a few pieces.

Rats are quick to exercise their mastery of climbing and balancing.

4. Of course rats can also jump, but they prefer to climb. That's why there's not much danger that they'll jump onto a free-standing table or the windowsill, but will easily climb up the cabinet walls. Doors, drawers, and cabinet doors should be kept closed during free exercise in order to prevent accidents.

5. While your rats are running around, it's best for you to remain seated with the telephone within reach so you don't have to jump up suddenly if it rings. Turn the ringer down low so it doesn't frighten the rats. Children should be instructed to take off their shoes when they enter the room and to be careful not to step on the rats.

Note: Never scold your rats if they have caused some damage while running around free. Rats don't understand what has suddenly gone wrong. In their view they have done absolutely nothing wrong.

How to Catch a Rat

Perhaps you need to leave the house in a hurry while the rats are running around. During your absence you want the rats in their cage. How can you get the rats back into their cage quickly? It's easy: Entice the little creatures with treats, pick them up, and return them to the cage. The trick is in the treats.

Many Rats Love to Bathe

Brown rats that live in the wild are outstanding swimmers. And many tame fancy rats are

The main thing is to hang on. Form doesn't count yet.

happy to take a bath, particularly in the summer. Pleasure in bathing has nothing to do with cleanliness, since rats groom just as enthusiastically as cats do. The fancy rat swimming pool is for cooling off or for exercise, and it's simply lots of fun for fancy rats.

In the summer, try placing a small plastic children's pool with lukewarm water in the sun for the rats to enjoy. You should stay nearby while they are bathing.

Since rats can't climb on the slick sides of the plastic water container without help, you'll have to give them a little support. Provide a small float, for example, made of pieces of cork, or get a small wooden ladder from your pet dealer

10 Golden Rules
for Fancy Rat Owners

1 Rats are happiest in the company of other rats. Therefore, it's best to have two animals right from the start.

2 From the first day, talk to the animals frequently and hold them on your lap or in your sweater. Rats need physical contact.

3 Never pick up a rat by its tail. Grasp it with two fingers under the chest and place your thumb on the back. Larger animals should also be supported with the other hand under their hindquarters (see illustration on page 22).

4 The best way for children to carry rats is with both hands around the rat's chest. But they mustn't squeeze too tightly.

5 Rats love exercise and are extremely eager to learn. Don't set excessively narrow limits to their free exercise, but make sure they are in surroundings that are safe for them.

6 Many rats never become housebroken, whether in the cage or romping around in the home. Don't be upset by small mishaps.

7 Yelling and scolding only push rats into a state of panic, since they are sensitive to noise. Avoid unnecessary noise.

8 See to it that the animals have lots of variety even in their cage and can keep very busy.

9 Rats are nibblers. They spread their mealtimes out over the full 24 hours. Leftover greens are often hidden in the sleeping house, where they rot. It's best to check that area regularly.

10 Don't feed your rat by hand until it has gotten used to you; otherwise it may bite. Rats need to be raised with lots of understanding, tolerance, and love.

and hang it in the water. Be sure to test the float to see if it will support the weight of a rat; take an object of about the same weight as the rat and place it on the float in the water.

It's best to fasten the float to the edge of the kiddy pool with strong wire so it doesn't scoot away when the rat wants to climb onto it. Now carefully place the rat into the water. If it enjoys paddling around, let it have fun for a few minutes. But if it acts fearful or tries to get out of the water, immediately lift it out. After the swim the rat will dry its fur in the sun.

In the winter and on cool days bathing should take place only in a heated room. After the bath, carefully rub the rat's fur with a soft towel and place the animal near a heater.

Note: If three or four attempts to get your rat to bathe convince you that the animal doesn't like the water, don't press the issue further.

Rats Like to Sun Themselves

Rats like warmth and sunshine, and the sun activates vitamin D, which combats rickets. So let your rat have a sunbath from time to time. The important thing is to let the rats decide for themselves how long they want to stay in the sun. Never set the cage in direct sunlight, since fancy rats, like other pets, can get heatstroke.

Note: Rats that get too little sun can experience a vitamin D deficiency and may be likely to catch colds.

Taking Your Rat for a Walk

You certainly can take your rat for a walk. Of course the animal first has to be used to you, and you have to practice with it inside the home. If you spend lots of time with your rat and frequently carry it around inside the house, then usually you can try the first walk after three to four weeks. Place the rat in your sleeve, or in the pocket of your pants, skirt, or

---

TIP

House Plants

Rats gnaw on everything available during their free exercise. Make sure that rats can't nibble on house plants. Poisonous plants include agaves, aloe, cyclamen, wake-robin, hemp, Christmas rose and holly, chrysanthemum, narcissus, dieffenbachia, ivy, angel's trumpet, ferns, fig trees, and flamingo flowers; also, unfortunately, geraniums, hydrangeas, hyacinths, crocuses, lilies of the valley, mistletoe, myrtle, narcissus, oleander, primrose, passion flowers, castor-oil plant, rhododendron, climbing rose, poinsettia, and calla lilies. For a complete list of harmful and poisonous plants, ask your veterinarian or local librarian.

---

jacket. If the rat is entirely at ease with you, you can also carry it on your shoulder. Rats are not inclined to assert their independence at the first opportunity, and as a rule they calmly remain right where they are. It is advisable to take walks with the creature in quiet areas in order to avoid any possible frightening situations. If a rat becomes panic-stricken, it will attempt to run away.

The greatest problem any time a rat runs away is the reaction of other people, who might be alarmed by rampant rats. The fancy rat owner needs to keep cool, and in some cases put up with people's reactions, ranging from aloof silence to anger. But in no case should you be overly concerned with individuals who are stuck in the Middle Ages and can think of nothing but the plague when they see a rat.

A basket nest is a welcome spot for a snooze.

Can Fancy Rats Be House-trained?

Every rat burrow in the wild has a secluded spot that the resident rats use as a toilet. After a certain time, the rats wall it up with dirt and other material.

Like all domesticated animals, rats have lost some of their wild ways. As a result, many fancy rats never become house-trained. Nevertheless, it's worthwhile in any case to try.

At the start of the daily free exercise, shortly after the rats leave the cage, they may frequently leave droppings. You can turn this tendency to good advantage by encouraging them to use the small travel cage as a toilet (see illustration on page 18).

It's a good idea to keep the toilet in the same place in the room. Provide absorbent paper on the cage floor and the accustomed bedding on top of that (see Cage Accessories, page 16). Place the animals in the travel cage for about ten minutes. This training device often works, but unfortunately there are some rats that never catch on.

Note: Rats are not always welcome in hotels and guest houses. Call ahead first to see if they are allowed.

Teaching Tricks

Fancy rats are intelligent creatures that thrive on interaction with their owner. Your pet needs at least an hour a day of your undivided attention. You might want to devote part of this time to teaching it a few tricks. Fancy rats can be taught to come when called, stand up to "beg," run to greet you, and even help you clean their cages.

The keys to training your rat are
✔ Trust
✔ Gentle handling
✔ No shouting or harsh corrections
✔ Consistency
✔ Repetition
✔ Individual attention
✔ Food rewards

Training Treats

After you have hand-tamed your pet and it has grown to trust you and to look forward to your time together, you can move on to more challenging activities. Using food as a reward almost always guarantees that a fancy rat will learn what its owner wants to teach it. Rice Krispies or Cheerios are tasty treats—low in fat, sugar, and protein, and small enough that a few pieces during training sections won't result in a fat rat.

Coming When Called

To teach your rat to come when called, hold a bit of cereal up to the bars of its cage while it is inside, and softly call its name. Be careful to hold the cereal out in front of your fingers, or it may consider a fingertip part of the treat and unintentionally bite you.

After a few days, your rat will associate its name with a treat. Now you can progress to doing the same outside the cage, giving the treat only when the rat has approached you at the sound of its name. After a few weeks, your pet will come when called, even without a treat, although you should continue to reinforce its behavior with an occasional treat.

Rats amuse themselves for hours with a small cardboard box.

Sitting Up

This trick is taught using the natural inclination of your rat to reach up for food. After your fancy rat has run up to you, hold a piece of cereal over its head so it has to stand on its hind legs to reach it. At the same time say "Up!" or a similar short command. After two weeks, your pet should respond to the command with or without its treat.

FANCY RATS HOME ALONE

Leaving fancy rats at home: *If some absolutely reliable friends or neighbors can take care of your pets in their familiar surroundings, that's the ideal solution. Carefully explain to your vacation replacement how to take care of the animals and feed them. The fancy rats and their rat sitter should have a chance to get to know each other beforehand. Of course, only people who like and understand rats should be considered for the job.*

Boarding the rats: *The best place is with a fellow rat fancier. Many pet shops and animal shelters will board rats for a while. They won't get the attention they're used to, and usually not the same food they get at home. So don't be surprised if your rats are afraid of strangers after you get back.*

Taking them along: *This can be recommended only in certain circumstances—for example, if you are traveling by car to a vacation home or apartment and can provide the accustomed necessities for the animals.*

Proper Nutrition

Rats need the right amount of nutritious food in order to stay fit.

Although omnivorous by nature, rats are primarily vegetarian, and prefer corn, nuts, fruit, and vegetables. The fat in corn feed and nuts gives them all the fat they need in their diet.

Staple Food for Rats

Your fancy rats should get a daily ration of colorful grain feed in their food dish; sunflower seeds and peanuts should be part of the mixture.

Guinea pig food from the pet store is a good choice. But it should be enriched by adding sunflower seeds, oats, millet, pieces of dried fruit, and dry pasta. Mix in some parrot food, and dry dog or cat kibble.

If you make your own grain mixture, the food must contain 70 percent grains. You'll have to experiment to determine what menu your rats prefer. The best proportion of oats is 20 percent; coarse oats are better than mealy instant oats. The remaining 10 percent of the feed should consist of small bits of various nuts and dried fruit.

Protein content is increased by sprinkling a teaspoonful of soy flour over the food. Small pieces of yeast (which contains B vitamins and protein) add to the nutritional content. The yeast should make up about 5 percent of the total quantity of food.

Note: Don't feed rats exclusively on grains. Because of their high content of phytic acids, they can cause rickets.

Food quantity: Medium-sized rats that weigh about 8 ounces (220 g) get about three-quarters of an ounce (22 g) of staple food. Larger rats need a correspondingly greater amount of food.

Lettuce and Vegetables

Rats are very fond of lettuce. If possible, get organic lettuce for the animals. Endive and dark leafy lettuces are the best kind. Rats also like dandelion greens and daisies. You can really make them happy with a bowl of cat grass.

With the exception of legumes, all types of vegetables are good for fancy rats. Examples include cauliflower, broccoli, cucumbers, corn, carrots, kohlrabi, celery, asparagus, and zucchini.

Note: Before feeding vegetables and lettuce, wash and dry them and serve them in a separate bowl.

Fruit for a Sweet Tooth

Fresh and dried fruits are a favorite treat for fancy rats; they contain many important vitamins and trace elements. But be careful with fruit that has a pit containing hydrocyanic acid. Remove the pit from apricots, plums, cherries, and peaches before you offer these fruits to your pet. On the other hand, apples, bananas, pears, strawberries, and raspberries are harmless.

Sprouts

Oat and wheat sprouts contain important vitamin E, which guards against fatty tissue diseases and inflammations. They should be served as frequently as possible. Cover the grain seeds with water and let them soak in a warm place for about 24 hours. Then sprout the seeds in flat, covered glass jars on the windowsill. Add a little water every day. In about five days the sprouts can be fed to your rats. Vitamin-E

deficiency can develop in the cold season, when there's not as much fresh food.

Further additions: Pieces of dark bread, crackers and various cereals found in your kitchen, plus some cooked egg yolk once a week; and from time to time some small bits of mild sliced cheese.

Animal Protein

In order to meet the minimal need of your fancy rats for animal protein, feed them fish flakes and freezed-dried brine shrimp available at pet stores. Another possibility is cooked fish fillets, boned and unseasoned. You can also give them small quantities of cooked ground beef mixed with cereal about once a week.

The two rats are alert as they stand guard.

Something to Gnaw

Since rats need continually to wear down their incisor teeth, there should always be some toasted, mold-free dark bread—no white bread—in the cage. For a change of pace you can also give the rats some hard toast made from whole-grain bread, and, at least four times per week, lab-blocks (compressed rodent food), which will supply the animals with all their nutritional needs.

Nuts in the shells should be part of your rat's diet. A hazelnut per day and a walnut every week are beneficial for their high fat content. Rats are also very fond of chestnuts and peanuts. Serve them both with the shell on. The little rodents, however, can't bite into the hard shells of Brazil nuts.

It's tough to choose from such a banquet.

The Appropriate Drink

Rats drink a lot of water. They also like to dip their feet into it.

Keep fresh water available at all times. A simple glass bottle with a ball valve in the drinking tube can be hung from the side of your fancy rat's cage.

Change the water daily and scrub the bottle thoroughly twice a week. If you use a plastic bottle, replace it every two or three months, because health-threatening bacteria and algae build up more easily on plastic than on glass surfaces.

Since fancy rats have become popular house pets, owners have found out that a water bottle alone is not the ideal arrangement. Many rat owners also place a dish on the top floor of the cage so that the water doesn't get dirty from the bedding. This dish should be heavy ceramic with a solid base. Change the water daily. Before refilling the dish, wash it with hot water to prevent algae—an ideal culture medium for bacteria.

Harmful Foods

Leftovers: Spices, including salt, contained in leftovers such as hot dogs, ham, and bacon can be harmful to a rat's health.

Sweets: In rats they can cause allergies and related disorders accompanied by terrible itching and damage to the coat. Chocolate is particularly dangerous, since it contains milk as well as sugar. Milk produces not only allergies in rats, but frequently diarrhea, too. It's best to give rats small pieces of fresh or dried fruit as a reward, or rodent fruit drops sold in pet stores.

Legumes expand in the rat's stomach and produce intestinal gas. Rats can die a painful death as a result. Raw and cooked peas and beans have no place in fancy rat food.

Butter: Large amounts of butter can be life threatening to rats.

Drinks: Alcohol, tea, coffee, cola, and lemonade should be considered taboo for fancy rats.

Note: You can give fancy rats cooked potatoes, rice, and pasta in small quantities, but with no added spices. Uncooked noodles are best.

Checklist
Feeding

1 Provide a variety of foods.

2 Feed regularly morning and evening.

3 Staple food: prepared corn feed for guinea pigs (see page 30). Supplemental foods: fruits, lettuce, and other vegetables (see page 31).
For gnawing: Hard dark bread or whole-grain toast, and nuts in their shells

4 Once a week, a little flaked fish food, cooked fish fillet, or hamburger (see page 31).

5 Provide greens in a separate food dish.

6 Always make fresh drinking water available.

7 For rewards, use small pieces of fruit and rodent fruit drops.

8 Harmful foods are leftovers, spices, sweets, alcohol, coffee, tea, lemonade, dog food, and cat food.

The Well-Cared-for Rat

Rats are easy to care for. Since they groom themselves thoroughly several times a day with their tongue, they don't need to be bathed or brushed. But be sure to check regularly:

✔ Incisor teeth; if they become too long, they get in the way when the rat tries to eat. Overgrown incisors must be shortened by the veterinarian. Hard chewing material helps make that unnecessary (see page 32).

✔ Nails: Even the claws sometimes need clipping, which is also done by the veterinarian. Nails that become too long are a hindrance when the rat runs.

Check your rat's incisors once a month.

As a preventive measure, you can let the rat run on a hard surface such as concrete from time to time.

✔ Eyes: A discharge from the nose or eyes is an indication of illness. So it's not enough to wipe the eyes or nose with a soft tissue; you should ask your veterinarian for advice.

✔ Rear: With occasional diarrhea that quickly disappears, gently clean the rat's rear end with warm water and a small cloth.

✔ Coat: Use warm water to wash matted areas in the fur caused by spilled food.

✔ Ears: Carefully soften crusty material in the ears with a dampened paper tissue (don't use cotton swabs).

A rat thoroughly washes itself from head to toe up to six times a day.

Cleaning the Cage and Accessories

A dirty cage and filthy accessories can make your rat sick, and produce unpleasant odors in your home. Bacteria cultures can build up and cause skin disorders, and vermin such as fleas and mites can find ideal breeding places. Do these chores as part of your routine:

Daily: Clean the food dish and water bottle with hot water. Check to see if the rats soil their sleeping house with droppings and urine. If they do, wash and line this area daily (see Sleeping House, page 17).

Every three days: Remove all bedding. Wash the floor and any soiled cage bars with hot water, and add fresh bedding.

Note: If you change the bedding frequently, your fancy rats will not get used to using one place as a toilet area (see Can Fancy Rats Be House-trained?, page 28).

Once or twice a week: Take the bedding out of the sleeping house and wash the house with hot water. Don't forget to line it again with fresh bedding once it's dry.

As needed: Wash toys, ladders, tubes, ramps, and similar accessories with hot water whenever they become soiled.

Bath time: While you're cleaning your fancy rats' cage, put a large, low water bowl on the floor and encourage them to splash to their hearts' content. By the time their cage is clean, they'll be clean, too, and won't bring any filth or odor back into their living area.

Note: Virtually all cleaning agents contain chemicals. Use nothing but hot water to clean the cage and accessories to protect the animals from poisons and allergens. If the cage gets filthy, use washing soap or soap flakes.

The best way to get rid of dead hairs is to stroke your fancy rat.

Petting Is Good for the Fur

Rats like to be petted by their owner. It's an easy way to get rid of dead hairs when the animals are shedding in the spring and fall. Place the rat on the floor or a table and stroke it carefully on the head, back, and flanks to loosen old hairs, and to make the coat stay glossy and as soft as silk.

Fancy Rats Multiply

Rats mature early and are incredibly prolific. On an average, rats reach sexual maturity at the age of six weeks and can be fully mature as young as four weeks. In every litter—one to eleven per year—a female rat can give birth to as many as 20 young. At 15 to 18 months, menopause occurs, and the female rat ceases to be fertile.

A Cautionary Note about Breeding

According to some estimates, on a worldwide scale, 1.5 to 3 rats are born for every human. That doesn't even take into consideration the rats that are bred for laboratory research. So what could possibly be more irresponsible than purposely breeding rats? But that's precisely what goes on. People have even come up with standards that describe exactly how various types of offspring should look, just as dog and cat fanciers have written standards for the breeds.

The acknowledged goal is to produce healthy animals and increase their

life expectancy. On the other hand, a more common goal is to breed more attractive rats with long or curly fur, and in stylish colors. No one seems to be asking if this is good or bad for the rats.

Previously it was thought that the natural life expectancy of rats was six to seven years. Recently that has come into question. Evidence to the contrary is that females become barren at the age of 15 to 18 months. In addition, rats that are two years old already show signs of aging:

✔ Movements become slower and more difficult.

✔ The animals start to get gray.

✔ Interest in playing and romping wanes noticeably.

For those reasons, it is unlikely that rats can be bred to live longer.

101 Fancy Rats?

Serious hobby breeders know how difficult it is to find homes even for popular animals such as dogs and cats. The mere thought that several times a year your desperate rat-owner friends are going to phone you looking for homes for their excess offspring is enough to make you break out in a cold sweat. Anyone who feels that's not a problem should first experiment by taking out a classified ad in the newspaper with the following message: "Free! Attractive, healthy young rats." Then wait and see how many serious inquiries come in. Many unwanted fancy rats end up in animal shelters, as snake food in the zoo, or on the street, where their lives are nasty, brutish, and

At birth, rats weigh between 1.4 and 3.5 ounces (40 to 100 g). Adult rats tip the scales at between 7 to nearly 18 ounces (200 to 500 g).

short because they are no longer suited to life in the wild.

If you want to spare animals that kind of fate, don't even think of breeding your pets.

Fancy Rat Birth Control

In order to prevent breeding, keep males and females in separate cages and let them run free at different times. That's not a permanent solution, because it unnecessarily frustrates the gregarious animals.

Neutering the male is the most reliable preventive measure; it must be performed only by a veterinarian who has experience with rats. Males can be altered at the age of eight weeks.

After neutering, wait two or three days as a precaution before putting the two sexes back together.

Rats carefully investigate everything to see if it's edible.

Note: If you accidentally acquire a female that is already pregnant, get in touch immediately with everyone you know, so you can find a good home for at least some of the young ones.

Pregnancy and Birth

Copulation: The female signals when she is ready to mate by producing sex hormones that attract the male. Females are in heat for six hours, and each coupling takes only a few seconds.

Gestation Period: Gestation lasts about 24 days. During this time and the following four

Don't pick up the babies, unless you think that one of them may be sick.

Starting in the fourth week of life you can begin carefully stroking the babies with one finger. But first stroke the mother so that she understands your good intentions.

Female rats are protective mothers. If they fear that their young are threatened, they can become very forceful and aggressive. Therefore, as a precautionary measure, keep children, visitors, and house pets far away from the nest. Treat the mother rat to some tasty snacks and kind words to lessen her anxiety.

How the Young Develop

Young rats, born blind and hairless, are slow to leave the nest.

Starting at the age of ten days young rats begin to grow fur.

Between the thirteenth and sixteenth day they open their eyes. As soon as they can see, they scramble out of the nest to explore their immediate surroundings. The mother herds them together and carries them back to the nest.

TIP

Separating Young Animals

Young rats can become sexually mature at four weeks, but the male can't be neutered until he is eight weeks old. Keep the young animals separated by sex for about a month. Have your veterinarian identify the sex. Place the males in their own cage; the females can stay with the mother. When the young males are out of their cage, the mother can be present the first two weeks, but later that would be too risky. In the world of rats, incest is not taboo. Twenty-four hours after neutering, the family can be put back together again.

---

weeks of nursing, double the amount of food and water you give the mother. Provide her with lots of good nutrition and variety.

Birth: Birth often takes place in the early morning hours. The experienced mother rat has already prepared a nest for her young. Since nest building is learned behavior, a new mother will simply place the young of her first litter anywhere in the cage. You have to help her by making a snug nest with soft tissues and fabric remnants. Young rats need lots of warmth, because they are born hairless.

Note: Mother rats are ready to conceive again only 15 to 24 hours after giving birth!

Female Rats Are Good Mothers

Leave the young rats to the care of their mother as long as she continues to suckle them. Rarely does a mother rat become ill or neglect her young.

Two and a half weeks after birth, start providing food for the young, even though most will still be suckling. Good choices include soy flower, crushed oat meal, oat flower, flax seed, baby food with fruits and vegetables, and tiny pieces of fruit, lettuce, and other vegetables.

At the age of four weeks some precocious rats will be sexually mature.

At five weeks the first coat of fur is completely grown in.

At six weeks the first shedding takes place. At this age all young animals are capable of reproducing.

Note: A mother rat will suckle her young for up to four weeks. But even after that there is a bond between mother and children for at least another two weeks. The young follow their mother everywhere and learn from her how to search for food and steer clear of danger.

Do Them a Favor

At this point, the young are almost ready to go to their new owners. Before you part with them, however, take them to the veterinarian to be spayed or neutered (see page 37) so they won't add to the multitude of unwanted rats whose owners, overwhelmed by sheer numbers as their pets multiply, drop them off at the animal shelter or, worse yet, abandon them outdoors, thinking they will adapt. Domesticated fancy rats probably cannot last more than a few days in the wild without starving, freezing, being run over by a car, or becoming prey for a cat, dog, or owl.

There can be 14 or more rats in a litter.

UNDERSTANDING YOUR FANCY RAT

Rats are very clever, playful, and adventurous creatures. In order to provide them a pleasant life, they need not only good care and affection from both rats and humans, but also lots of exercise and stimulation to keep busy.

Brown Rats

To understand your fancy rat's behavior, you need to know about the habits of its wild ancestors. Brown rats live together in packs or family clans. The extended family includes the great-grandfather as well as cousins six times removed. They all get along. Squabbles are exceptionally rare. Every animal willingly accepts the tasks assigned to it. Even reproduction takes place essentially within the clan. Nevertheless, that does not produce evidence of inbreeding. Because of the fecundity of the female, there is no lack of partners that are not close blood relatives. On the other hand, females often prefer sexual partners from the immediate family. Relationships with other rat clans are distant but not hostile, since rats are peaceful animals. In addition, they can always avoid each other in the wild.

Life in a Rat Colony

Underground rat dens in the wild are laid out in a sophisticated and complicated way.

Rats love to climb on ladders. This young one is having a little trouble hanging on.

A **rat colony** contains several rooms that serve distinct purposes, a number of passageways, and several entrances and exits.

Inside the rat colony are storerooms, sleeping chambers, living rooms, a toilet, and an especially safe room in the middle of the burrow for nursing rats. The older dominant males, young animals, and females that have not yet started suckling stay in the adjacent chambers around the nursery. At the outer edge of the colony, in the less secure areas, live the young, adolescent, and adult family members. It seems that the clan is prepared to cope in times of danger with the possible loss of these animals first.

Pecking Order

The pecking order among rats is not as iron-clad as with most other animals. In a pride of lions, for example, it is presumed that the older, dominant males have first crack at feeding. Weaker, younger animals and females have to make do with meager leftovers. But with rats the situation is reversed. If there's not enough food to satisfy everyone, the stronger males yield to the younger animals and the females.

The highest ranking male rats are tolerant and overlook quite a lot. Their main task is to protect the extended family from enemies and other dangers. Life in a rat colony seems to be characterized by mutual affection and consideration.

The animals willingly and generously help one another in caring for their coats, and they snuggle close together when they sleep. An activity known as crawling over and under seems to be a pleasant pastime for old and young family members. Older rats crawl over the younger ones, apparently in a show of mutual affection.

Dividing Duties

The young males and females that live on the edges of the colony have the special assignment of warning the clan whenever danger threatens. They sound a high-frequency alarm, run into the inner chambers of the living quarters, and wake everyone up.

The highest ranking older males then decide how to combat the danger. They go out prepared to do battle with an intruder. If necessary, they arrange for and organize a retreat from the burrow.

Usually the sexually mature females are occupied with raising their young.

Female rats raise their young together in the protected nursery. There are no boundaries dividing birthing nests. If one of the females leaves the room to look for food or for some other purpose, the others take care of her young in her absence. They suckle, groom, and watch over the young rats along with their own, assuring the survival of the little rats even if something should happen to the mother outside and she doesn't return.

Building a nest is behavior that rats have to learn. In natural conditions in the pack, the young females look to the experienced ones to see how it's done. They rarely get involved in defending the nest against intruders unless there is no male support available.

Young male rats usually function as tasters for the clan. They perform a very important and dangerous task. It falls to them to be the first ones to taste unknown foods—a piece of pizza, an exotic fruit, or even a new poison bait. The other animals observe the taster attentively and wait to see what happens. Not one approaches the food, even if food is scarce. Only after several hours have gone by without the taster showing signs of illness or dying do the other rats dig into the food.

Your rats can make a cozy place to snuggle out of an old towel.

Young rats accept only food that older animals have already gnawed and that bears traces of their scent. This refined technique has contributed to the survival of rats. No member of a rat clan will ever touch any bait that has caused the death of a taster. It's hard to decide which to admire more, the long memory of all the other rats, or the courage of the tasters who risk their lives for the benefit of the others.

A Fancy Rat's Day

If everything is normal, no particular danger threatens, and the food supply is assured, the exceptionally curious rat spends around 80 percent of its active time exploring its surroundings.

Rats sniff everything they encounter. They do this not only out of curiosity, but also because of caution. Every change in their surroundings is carefully noted, and everything is suspicious. Rats smell a trap—in the literal or figurative sense—at every departure from the norm.

Rats spend the rest of their time painstakingly grooming their fur. They clean themselves, preferably in the sun, until every individual hair positively shines. More of their time is taken up with gnawing to wear down their incisor teeth, which never stop growing. There's still time for exchanging affection with one another and for satisfying their sex drive.

TIP

Playground for Rats

Many of the innate abilities that animals have developed through thousands of years of evolution atrophy in the care of humans, simply because they are no longer needed. That can't be entirely avoided; but even if your fancy rats don't keep busy with the tasks of their forebears, you can at least be sure that they don't suffer from boredom. With a little modification, an old kitchen table that's no longer used can easily be converted into a playground for rats (see illustration, pages 50–51). Place it in the middle of the room. To keep the playground apparatus (seesaws, ramps, ladders, and tubes) from falling off the table, fasten a chipboard edge around the table. You can craft a frame about 6 inches (15 cm) high that you can lift off with a handle. For longer visits by the rats you can also put one or two sleeping houses into the playground.

Note: More ideas for fancy rat fun are in the How-to section on pages 48 and 49.

Signal of danger: The rat stands up and emits a cry that's inaudible to humans.

FANCY RAT
BEHAVIOR

This is how rats communicate with one another and with their owners.

 My rat displays this behavior.

 What's the rat trying to tell me?

 How to react to its behavior!

 The rat spends a lot of time washing itself with its tongue.

? Rats carefully groom their fur several times every day.

! Never disturb the animal while it's grooming.

The rat sniffs the air with raised snout.

? It's fearful. Is there any danger?

! You can calm the animal by talking reassuringly to it.

Rats like to lie together.

? They need physical contact.

! Frequently hold your rat on your lap.

The rat checks out its friend's bottom.

? The rat's specific scent tells the others if the rat is part of the family.

! Don't wash your hands or put on cologne before picking up your rat.

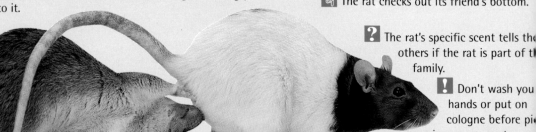

The treat is devoured with pleasure.

Food stimulates a rat's willingness to learn.

Treats help you hand-tame your pet.

Standing on hind legs provides a better view.

Something has stimulated the rat's curiosity.

Speak softly and calmly to the rat.

Friendly contact.

Rats need to be with their own kind.

Provide a large cage that's set up to provide lots of variety.

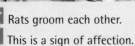

Rats groom each other.

This is a sign of affection.

Consider having more than one fancy rat.

If the Colony Gets Crowded

Lack of space is the only thing in the wild, besides natural disasters such as earthquakes or flooding, and manmade catastrophes such as excavation, that can cause rats to leave their den or territory. Not even a lack of food can force them to flee.

The younger rats leave their posts on the edges of the den and wander about in small groups in search of another place for a colony.

As they leave their home and travel for miles over unfamiliar terrain, the young rats are subject to a high rate of mortality from predators. Counterbalancing this is their prodigious rate of reproduction. A female is capable of conceiving within less than 24 hours of giving birth to a litter of as many as 14 baby rats. The larger the litter, the greater the chance that some will survive to adulthood. When a new site is found, the colony is quickly populated, and the migratory cycle repeats itself.

Domesticated rats don't have this opportunity if their cage becomes too small for them because of a growing population. If your pets are not transferred to another cage in a timely fashion, the younger animals form cliques and lose interest in the opposite sex. If things remain tight in the cage, even the older rats suddenly stop reproducing. Selfishness takes the place of the social behavior that's so highly developed in rats. Each animal lives its own life and tries whenever possible to secure its own privileges, such as a protected sleeping place. Often rats defend their interests by fighting. It's interesting that with a reduction in population following the natural death of a number of rats, this behavior doesn't change. No new socialization takes place, and the pack dies out.

Climbing straight up is easy for rats. The tail helps the rat hang on.

Voice and Body Language

How Rats Communicate	What It Means
Touch each other with the nose	Greeting
Stand on the hind legs and arch the back	This posture is often assumed at the start of grooming.
Stand on hind legs	Increased attentiveness
Nose stretched forward	The rat has caught a scent.
Stand on hind legs, mouth open so that the teeth are visible	Defensive posture. The rat is trying to look threatening in the presence of an antagonist; it emits a cry that's inaudible to humans (see illustration, page 43).
Sniff bottom or nose	Identifying family member or stranger
Pound on one another with front paws	Fighting behavior toward a strange rat
Older rats crawl over or under young ones several times	Exchange of affection
Cuddle together	Indicative of distinctive social contact
Mark	The territory is marked with urine.
Pick up hunks of food with front paws	At first the food is turned around in the paws to check it out carefully.
Hold out specific parts of the body, such as chin or upper body, to another rat	Invitation to groom one another
Extend the head	Increased wariness
Whistle	High, clear cry emitted when a rat is alarmed or angry. People with acute hearing perceive a whistling sound.

Play Stairs

A stimulating play area can be set up on seldom-used cellar stairs. Connect the steps with wooden ramps made from small boards or ceramic pipes your fancy rats can crawl through. On one step, put a bowl with cat grass or sand in it; on another step, a few small paper balls. On one side you can anchor a board covered with burlap.

In the staircase play area you can treat your pets to fresh vegetables, fruit, and lettuce.

Stretching Out in a Hammock

A hammock can be crafted from an old shirt or some other piece of fabric. At the narrow end, stitch the fabric to make a hem. Insert a small stick through the hem at each end and anchor the ends of the sticks horizontally on the outside of the cage bars, preferably in a corner. Be sure that the construction will hold your rat's weight. Place a pedestal or small step nearby so the rats can easily climb into the hammock.

These curious rats thoroughly investigate the old boot and use it as a cozy hideout.

Digging in the Sand

Rats have as much fun playing in sand as children do. The larger the plastic or metal container, the better. For additional stimulation you can hide some peanuts in the shell in the sand.

Climbing Ropes

Every cage should have a free-hanging climbing rope. Daily climbing excursions keep your little pets fit.

Paper and Cardboard

Favorite playthings of fancy rats include crumpled-up newspaper, paper towels, and wrapping paper. Cardboard boxes are also very popular. When they're worn out, they can simply be thrown away. Cardboard tubes from paper towels and toilet paper make snug hiding places.

How Rats Keep in Shape

Clever rats need lots of activity and variety to offset their dull existence in the cage. That's why you should:

✔ Keep more than one rat, if possible.
✔ Let the rat have lots of free exercise and cuddling.
✔ Set the cage up so that it offers lots of opportunities to play.
✔ Always provide surprises and variety.

Over time, things can get boring even in such nicely equipped cages with seesaws, tubes, ramps, and rope ladders. Don't wait until things go that far. Keep changing one piece of play apparatus for another.

For rats, physical contact with their own kind and with their owner is very important.

Rats Like Music

Remember the Pied Piper of Hamlin? He used a flute to lure the rats out of the city. Perhaps this story was based on the fact that rats really do like flute music—especially by Mozart. Music is useful in helping rats feel at ease if you have to leave them alone for a while, or simply in providing them pleasure. Just remember that since rats are sensitive to noise, they like only music that's played softly.

A Bit of Nature

Branches will occupy your rats for quite a while. They scratch and gnaw on them with gusto. But don't rip branches from a tree; pick up ones that have fallen to the ground.

Peel the bark off, because insects or their eggs might be lodged underneath. Before putting the branch in your rat's cage, immerse it in boiling water for 10 minutes to sterilize it. Some woods might be toxic to your pet. Check with your veterinarian, local library, experienced fancy rat owners, or garden club.

Climbing Poles for Steeplejacks

Pet stores have had climbing poles for cats for a long

Hollowed-out logs like this are available at pet stores. Rats like to gnaw on them and hide inside.

time. Fancy rats find them intriguing, too. Choose a climbing pole covered with sisal rather than carpeting. Set up the climbing pole away from cupboards and bookcases if you'd prefer that your pets not investigate your books, china, and knickknacks.

Note: Anchor the climbing pole well so that it can't fall over!

A stimulating rat playground. A hanging ladder and a wooden ladder invite the rats to climb and balance; the little house and the tubes are snug hiding places. Vegetables and fruit provide snacks.

Sense Perception in Rats

Senses, except sight, are very highly developed in fancy rats.

The sense of smell may be the most highly developed. Rats make use of a highly developed scent language. By checking another rat's rear end and sniffing its nose, they can distinguish between friend and foe. Individual pack members are also distinguishable from one another by their specific scent.

Also, a female that's ready to mate signals her receptivity with pheromones that create a "scent note."

Marking with urine is also part of the scent language. That's how a territory is staked out, or an escape path marked for the other pack members. Most important, fancy rats use their sense of smell to find their food.

Note: Rats learn to recognize their owner by that person's individual scent. That's why it's important to avoid washing your hands or using cologne before picking up a rat. The animal might not be able to detect your individual scent.

The sense of taste is also highly differentiated. It makes it possible for rats to detect even two parts per million of poison in a bait.

Hearing: There can be no doubt that rats have a language of their own. They communicate with one another in high-frequency registers. If they become angry, they emit high, clear cries that can be perceived by people with acute hearing, and

that could easily be mistaken for whistling (see illustration on page 43). In addition, there are special mating calls and the famous humility cry that rats use to signify surrender. When frightened, baby rats make squeaking sounds in the realm of ultrasound.

The sense of touch is of great help to the animals in finding their way. Their whiskers are especially sensitive.

The sense of sight is less acute than the other senses, as in the case of all other animals that are active at dusk and during the night.

The sense of balance is not yet very well understood. It's believed that with the aid of their sense of balance, rats are capable of predicting earthquakes and other natural disasters, much like living seismographs.

Amazing Abilities

Rats display some amazing sensory capabilities, and are capable of some surprising feats.

An old table that's not being used can be turned into a terrific playground for rats (see page 43).

✔ Adult rats can stretch themselves out and squeeze through openings no larger than a silver dollar.

✔ Rats can swim for miles, and can even fish well with their prehensile paws.

✔ Rats are very accomplished underwater swimmers; for example, they navigate easily through sewer canals.

✔ Rats can climb vertically in sewer pipes; for example, from the cellar up to the tenth floor of a high-rise building.

✔ Rats are true tightrope artists that can reach a desired destination by means of ships' lines, anchor chains, cables, or telegraph wires.

✔ Rats can adapt to any climate.

The Intelligence of Rats

The aptitude and adaptability of rats are proof of their intelligence. They can immediately find their way around in a totally strange environment and adapt to the new conditions.

Domestic rats have even changed their attitude toward humans, who for thousands of years did nothing but persecute them. They quickly become hand tame and cuddle with the owner as if he or she were nothing more than an oversized rat. But the most convincing evidence of their intelligence is their ability to survive. Surely their tough past as hunted and persecuted creatures plays a major role in that ability.

Any rat in the clan that was a slow learner and couldn't adapt to often adverse conditions had no chance of survival. Usually only the cleverest, most highly evolved animals were able to cope properly with any situation that arose.

Further signs of the intelligence of rats are their great social cooperation, and the support and defense they provide for one another. If rats were self-centered loners they would have been exterminated centuries ago.

HEALTH CARE AND ILLNESSES

By nature rats are quite hardy. You can support their strong constitutions by taking care of your fancy rats properly, feeding them the right foods, and providing them with plenty of exercise and relief from the boredom of living in a cage.

Prevention

Prevention is better than cure in dealing with illnesses.

Pay attention to the following:

✔ Give your rats a varied diet (see page 30).
✔ Protect them from drafts.
✔ Give your rats plenty of exercise (see page 24).
✔ Let them bask in the sun frequently (see page 27).
✔ Provide a protected, warm cage for them.

That's the best way to take care of your animals' health. Of course the rats may become ill despite your precautions. In this case, consult a veterinarian without delay.

Note: Don't try to diagnose the illness yourself and prescribe medicines for your fancy rats. Medicines that have worked for people, or that have been given to other house pets without ill effect, can be fatal to rats.

Homeopathic medicines have often worked with ill rats. Your veterinarian is the best judge of which course to take: natural herbs and essential oils, or pharmaceutical remedies.

Rats use their forepaws like hands. They turn bits of food about in their paws to examine them.

Choosing the Right Veterinarian

Especially in the case of fancy rats, it's essential to find the right veterinarian. You need an expert in small animals. But even there you have to be careful. Not every veterinarian understands rats. It's best to find a veterinarian experienced with rats even before you get an animal. Pet stores, local humane societies, and experienced rat owners can provide that type of information. Or simply phone the veterinarians in your area one by one and ask if they have had experience treating fancy rats.

Taking a Rat to the Veterinarian

A plastic travel cage is ideal; various models are available (see page 18). You can also transport a sick rat in a sturdy box with a cover. Drill some air holes in the top. Lay some papers in the bottom, and cover them with bedding.

In the winter you have to be sure that the rat is warm enough during transport. A regular warm water bottle will serve the purpose. Put the warm water bottle in a large box and set the smaller box containing the sick animal on top of it.

Here are the early signs of illness:

✔ Loss of appetite

✔ No interest in exercise

✔ Diarrhea

✔ Dull or dry fur, oily scabs, bloody or crusty spots in the fur

✔ Sneezing, coughing, or rattling while breathing

✔ Protruding growths

✔ Changes in behavior, such as apathy and fear of strangers

If one or more symptoms of illness appear, follow this rule of thumb: observe your rat for a day. If the symptoms disappear in this time frame, all is well. But if not, you must go to the veterinarian right away. It's pointless for you to try to play doctor; the same symptoms could indicate a cold, for example, or lung cancer.

Note: A rat might suddenly bite you while you're petting it. In tame rats, this behavior can be indicative of a health problem. Probably your touch is causing the animal pain. So don't pick up a sick rat any more frequently than you have to.

Common Illnesses

Common illnesses are the illnesses that most frequently affect fancy rats. Of course, there are a number of other possible sicknesses. Whenever you have any doubts, go directly to the veterinarian.

The Primary Cause of Death: Cancer

Cancer seems to strike pet rats frequently at about the age of two years. One reason for this could be that our domestic rats are descended from laboratory animals that were intentionally bred to have a susceptibility to cancer, and were used in research to find a cure for humans afflicted with forms of that disease.

Tumors appear primarily on the legs and flanks; internal organs are rarely stricken with cancer. These first outer swellings are operable, but there's a high probability that new swellings will appear not many months later. So an operation could extend the animal's life, but only for a short time. Rats that are stricken with cancer usually retain their appetite and behave quite normally. In the advanced stages they become emaciated, lose interest in their surroundings, and suddenly die.

Diarrhea

Symptoms: Soft or runny droppings, matted bottom, loss of appetite. The rat's condition deteriorates very quickly through rapid loss of fluids and minerals.

Possible causes: Nutritional problem (e.g., too much fruit), infections.

Treatment: Diarrhea is harmless as long as it ceases within 24 hours. During this

*Overweight animals
are more susceptible
than thin ones
to cancer.*

Recognizing Sickness

Early Signs	Possible Causes	Treatment
Sneezing, wet nose	Cold (see page 56)	Consult veterinarian.
Sneezing, wet nose, coughing, rattling	Inflammation of lungs, lung cancer (see pages 54, 56)	Consult veterinarian.
Diarrhea	Nutritional deficiency, infection	Consult veterinarian. Give fluids.
Bald, crusty, bloody patches in fur, oily scabs	Skin disease, fungus, parasites, or allergies (see pages 57 and 58)	Consult veterinarian.
Frequent scratching, red patches in fur, loss of fur	Allergies (see page 58), especially in albino rats	Remove hay, wood shavings, and blooming plants; consult veterinarian.
Frequent scratching, white spots in fur, scabs	Parasites (mites, lice, etc.; see page 58)	Consult veterinarian.
Abscesses (see page 57)	Minor injuries	Consult veterinarian.
Large swellings, principally on legs and flanks	Cancer (see page 54)	Consult veterinarian.
Loss of appetite	Various illnesses	Change food; have veterinarian examine rat.
Injuries	Bites from other rats, accidents	Consult veterinarian.
Excessive thirst	Kidney disorder, possibly leptospirosis (see page 56)	Consult veterinarian.

time, feed the rat nothing. Have young animals under six months immediately treated by the veterinarian. In adult rats, diarrhea that lasts more than a day should also be treated by the veterinarian. It's best to take a fresh stool sample in a clean, closed container.

Immediate measures: Provide plenty of fluids for the sick rat. Chamomile or fennel teas are better than water in this instance. Holding the rat on your lap, dribble some into the rat's mouth with a syringe from which you've removed the needle.

Colds

Symptoms: Sneezing, coughing, rattling breath, wet nose

Possible cause: The cage is located in a drafty place.

Treatment: Go to the veterinarian right away, since the same symptoms can be caused by lung disorders such as inflammation of the lungs or lung cancer. Even in the case of a mere cold there's not much sense in treating the sick animal with home remedies such as chamomile steam or heat lamp therapy.

Prevention: Prevent colds by providing warm nesting material, and be sure that the cage is free of drafts.

Leptospirosis

Fancy rats kept as house pets rarely come into contact with pathogens that infect wild rats. That applies to Leptospirosis pathogens, which cause a severe infection. Just the same, you have to be very careful and use strict hygiene practices. If your rats run around in your yard, be sure it is free of feces from other animals.

Symptoms: Excessive thirst. Since this sickness is communicable to humans, especially through bites, you should not let your rats run around outdoors unless you know the area is absolutely clean. When they need fresh air, it's a better idea to set them in their cage on a table in a shady place in your yard.

Treatment: Take the rat to a vet. Usually the illness is harmless to the rat.

Leptospirosis appears most commonly in dogs, which, unlike rats, can be vaccinated against it.

Rats are happiest in the company of other rats.

Fungal Infections

Fungal infections in fancy rats are quite unlikely. But these infections are communicable to people. The most widespread is bald scab or trichophytosis (microspora).

Symptoms: Circular or oval patches where hair has fallen out, with slightly swollen border, surrounded by inflamed skin.

Causes: Fungi that may have been brought in on bedding and food.

Treatment: Avoid all contact with contaminated sites, since bald scab is highly contagious. Go straight to the veterinarian and pay particular attention to hygienic measures. If necessary, also go to your own dermatologist.

Note: Other fungal illnesses are possible.

Young rats learn by observing their mother. They follow wherever she goes.

Abscesses

Symptoms: Small swellings that often become inflamed. Other signs are fever, pain, and pus.

Possible causes: Bites from other rats; scratches and other minor injuries.

Treatment: The veterinarian should decide what to do in individual cases. Sometimes abscesses can be opened and drained, then treated with antibiotics.

Sick Fancy Rats

Sick rats need quiet and warmth more than anything else. Separate them for a while from their healthy cagemates if there is danger of infection. Ask the veterinarian if keeping a heat lamp near the cage makes any sense.

If the sick animal suffers from loss of appetite, offer it a diet of commercial baby food, without meat, but with carrots and other vegetables (also good for nursing rats back to health after giving birth, or after an operation).

Take good care of the sick rat. If you have to give up petting it because the animal doesn't want to be touched or because there is a danger of infection, spend some time talking softly to it. That will be comforting.

When you cannot be in the room, leave your radio on, playing classical music at low volume.

Allergies

First symptoms: Dull or dry fur, bloody or scaly spots in fur, bald spots in fur, loss of hair, frequent scratching.

Possible causes: Allergic reactions to chemically treated bedding such as hay or wood chips, fertilized vegetables, fruits, and lettuce, blooming house plants, and cleaning agents.

Treatment: Take the rat to a veterinarian to find out what is causing the allergy, even though that is often hard to determine. Then eliminate the causes.

External Parasites

Symptoms: Restless behavior, frequent scratching, white spots in the fur.

Possible causes: Mites, lice, fleas, ticks, or other parasites. Contamination results from direct contact with infested animals.

Treatment: These parasites can be eliminated with commercial preparations available in pet stores or from your veterinarian. Follow the directions exactly.

Liquids or ointments are more effective than powders or sprays, which can be inhaled or irritate the eyes. At the same time you treat the rat, thoroughly clean the cage, and change the bedding.

Baths in a commercial solution are effective against some parasites—much to the displeasure of the infested animal. The tiny, often brownish-black fleas, as well as lice, ticks, and other parasites, can survive on cage bars, ceramic tubes, and other accessories. So in conjunction with the bath cure, cage and furnishings must be thoroughly cleaned and disinfected.

Excessively Long Incisors

Symptoms: The rat's incisors, which continually grow, have become so long that the animal has trouble eating.

Cause: Lack of material to gnaw on.

Treatment: The veterinarian uses clippers to trim the teeth to the proper length. Have the veterinarian show you how it's done so that you can perform this simple procedure. Generally the rat won't try to defend itself too energetically once it realizes that you are trying to help it. Talk softly to it as you clip, and reward it with a treat afterwards.

Prevention: Always give your rats enough hard bread, nuts in the shell, and pieces of wood to gnaw so they can wear down their teeth.

Old-age Blindness

Many rats go blind when they get older. There's nothing that even the best veterinarian can do about that. But the animals get around amazingly well despite this handicap. They use their senses of hearing and balance to get their bearings. You have to be careful not to frighten them, and you should not surprise them by grabbing them from behind. Sometimes other rats will guide them by bumping them in the right direction. Hold your hand in front of the animal's nose so it can detect your scent before you touch it or pick it up. Speak to it softly.

Euthanizing Your Pet

If a fancy rat is suffering from an incurable illness and is clearly in considerable pain, you and your veterinarian should decide if it's best to euthanize your pet.

It would be cruel to make the animal continue to suffer. This has to be explained to children, who are often very attached to their beloved playmate. It's acceptable to bury a rat in your yard as long as it's buried at least 20 inches (50 cm) deep. Children might want to mark their pet's grave with a special stone.

The Empty Cage

If you've enjoyed having a fancy rat as a pet, you'll probably want to get another. The empty cage won't be empty for long if you contact one of the rat organizations that rescues and relocates unwanted pet rats (see Information, page 62). Most responsible rat breeders will make room in their homes for unwanted pet rats whose owners have abandoned them, usually because they didn't have time to care for them properly.

Fancy Rat Rescue

If you adopt a second-hand fancy rat, be prepared to give it extra time to overcome its initial shyness and learn to trust you. It may have had a traumatic experience with a previous owner, and will need more love, attention, and patience than a pet that has come to you directly from a reputable breeder.

It can be rewarding to provide a loving, permanent home to a needy fancy rat. But don't take on this responsibility until you have already gained experience by owning and training one or more well-socialized rats.

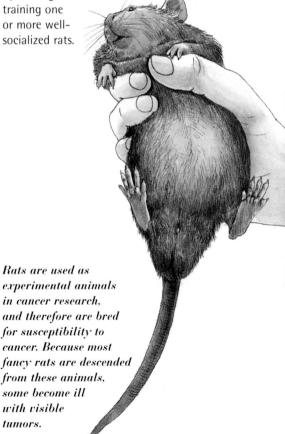

Rats are used as experimental animals in cancer research, and therefore are bred for susceptibility to cancer. Because most fancy rats are descended from these animals, some become ill with visible tumors.

A favorite activity of fancy rats is crawling over and under one another.

Fancy Rat Organizations
American Fancy Rat and Mouse Association
9230 64th Street
Riverside, CA 92509-5924
http://www.afrma.org

Rat and Mouse Club of America
55 Valley View Drive
Fitchburg, MA 01420-2138
webmaster@rmca.org

Books on Fancy Rats
Himsel, Carol A., DVM. *Rats: A Complete Pet Owner's Manual.* Barron's Educational Series, Inc., Hauppauge, New York: 1991.
Mays, Nick, *Your First Fancy Rat.* TFH Publications, Neptune City, New Jersey: 1996.

Magazine
Rat and Mouse Gazette
55 Valley View Drive
Fitchburg, MA 01420-2138
RMGazette@aol.com

Also Consult
  Your pet store owner, your veterinarian, and local and regional animal shelters and humane societies.

The Author
  Dr. Gisela Bulla, archeology Ph.D., lecturer, and freelance writer since 1976, is an activist animal protectionist and opponent of animal research. She is author of numerous animal books about cats, rats, and pet ownership.

The Translator
  Eric A. Bye, M.A., is a freelance translator working in German, French, Spanish, and English from his office in Vermont.

The Photographer
  Christine Steimer has worked since 1985 as a freelance photographer. Since 1989 she has specialized in animal photography and has worked for the German magazine *Das Tier (Animal)*.

The Illustrator
  György Jankovics studied art at the Art Academies of Budapest and Hamburg. He does animal and plant illustrations for a number of noteworthy publishers.

Editorial Consultants
  Matthew M. Vriends, Ph.D. and Dan Rice, D.V.M.

Photos: Book Cover and Inside

Front cover: This fancy rat's appeal is evident for all to see. It would love to be carried around on the shoulder of its owner. Rats come in a variety of attractive colors.

Page 1: Rats are primarily vegetarians. A pet rat should get a serving of cooked egg just once a week.

Pages 2–3: During free exercise in the home, put house plants in a safe place as a precaution. Rats are curious and could nibble on plants that are toxic to them.

Pages 4–5: Close physical contact with other rats is an ideal situation.

Pages 6–7: Friendship between a rat and a young, inexperienced kitten is a possibility, but it's unusual. Cats normally regard rats as prey. If you try this, stay nearby!

Page 64: Young rats already practice climbing.

Important Note

This book deals with keeping and taking care of fancy rats. In unsanitary conditions rats can become infested with skin fungi that are transferable to humans (see page 57); and people can also become infected with leptospirosis pathogens (see page 56).

Take a sick animal immediately to the veterinarian, and consult your doctor with any suspicions you may have about your own health. When you buy an animal, pay particular attention to symptoms of fungal skin disease (see page 57).

Rats are rodents that must be supervised during their necessary, regular free exercise in the home. In order to prevent life-threatening electrical shocks, be sure that the rats cannot gnaw any electrical cords.

English translation © Copyright 1999 by Barron's Educational Series, Inc.

© Copyright 1998 Grafe und Unzer Verlag GmbH, Munich

Original title of the book in German is *Ratten*

Translation from the German by Eric A. Bye

All inquiries should be addressed to:
Barron's Educational Series, Inc.
250 Wireless Boulevard
Hauppauge, New York 11788
http://www.barronseduc.com

Library of Congress Catalog Card No. 99-10570

International Standard Book No. 0-7641-0940-5

Library of Congress Cataloging-in-Publication Data
Bulla, Gisela.
    [Ratten. English]
    Fancy rats / Gisela Bulla ; photography, Christine Steimer ; drawings, György Jankovics.
       p. cm. — (Complete pet owner's manual)
    Includes bibliographical references and index.
    ISBN 0-7641-0940-5
    1. Rats as pets. I. Title. II. Series.
    SF459.R3B8513   1999
    636.9'352—dc21   99-10570
                                CIP

Printed in China

9 8 7 6 5 4 3 2

EXPERT ADVICE

An expert answers the ten most common questions about keeping fancy rats.

1 Can a fancy rat that's kept alone be happy?

2 Do males get along together as well as females?

3 Can you keep rats and mice together in the same cage?

4 How long have people been keeping fancy rats as house pets?

5 Can fancy rats be housebroken?

6 Are fancy rats expensive?

7 How long does it take for a fancy rat to become tame?

8 How much free exercise in the home do fancy rats need?

9 Can you keep fancy rats in an open-air enclosure?

10 Can you feed fancy rats leftovers?